Inspiring | Educating | Creating | Entertaining

Brimming with creative inspiration, how-to projects, and useful information to enrich your everyday life, Quarto Knows is a favourite destination for those pursuing their interests and passions. Visit our site and dig deeper with our books into your area of interest: Quarto Creates, Quarto Cooks, Quarto Homes, Quarto Lives, Quarto Drives, Quarto Explores, Quarto Gifts, or Quarto Kids.

First Published in 2021 by Wide Eyed Editions,
an imprint of The Quarto Group.
100 Cummings Center, Suite 265D, Beverly, MA 01915 USA.
T +1 978-282-9590 F +1 978-283-2742 www.QuartoKnows.com

A catalogue record for this book is available from the British Library.

ISBN 978-0-7112-5204-2

The illustrations were created digitally
Set in Arial Rounded MT Bold

Published by Georgia Amson-Bradshaw
Designed by Sasha Moxon
Edited by Georgia Amson-Bradshaw
Production by Dawn Cameron

Manufactured in Guangdong, China CC032021

9 8 7 6 5 4 3 2 1

# It's OK to Need a Friend

WIDE EYED EDITIONS

Everybody needs a friend.

Friends lift each other up.

"What a beautiful picture,
Owl!" says Little Brown Bear.

We all get into difficulty sometimes. But most problems can be solved if we ask our good friends for help.

"Hold on tight, Fox!"

Remember, it's OK to cry.

Good friends know that sometimes,
a hug says all there is to say.

We all make mistakes.
Sometimes we hurt each other.

It's what we do next
that matters.

"I'm so sorry, Mouse,"
says Little Brown Bear.

What else do good friends do?
Good friends listen.

Being heard warms
the heart like a
roaring fire.

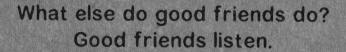

Sometimes our friends
have different needs
and feelings to us.

That can be hard
to understand.

Good friends love
each other for
who they are.

When we share happiness with our friends, we end up with more than we had in the beginning.

"Thank you for this delicious
acorn, Little Brown Bear!"
says Squirrel.

Little Brown Bear knows that to have good friends, you have to be a good friend.

"I love you all," says Little Brown Bear.

"And we love you too!" say his friends.